S0-CTX-335

Formentera

Followed by

The Gardens of Suzhou

Formentera
is the thirty-fifth volume
in the *Essential Poets* Series
published by Guernica Editions.

BERT SCHIERBEEK

Formentera

Followed by

The Gardens of Suzhou

Translated by Charles McGeehan

Guernica Editions

Original titles:
Formentera and *De Tuinen van Suzhou.*

Copyright © 1984, 1986 by Bert Schierbeek and De Bezige Bij
Translation © 1989 by Charles McGeehan and Guernica Editions
All rights reserved

Typesetting by compositions LHR
Printed in Canada

Guernica Editions, P.O. Box 633, Station N.D.G.
Montréal, Québec, Canada, H4A 3R1

Legal Deposit — First Quarter
Bibliothèque nationale du Québec & National Library of Canada

Canadian Cataloguing in Publication Data

Schierbeek, Bert, 1918
Formentera: The Gardens of Suzhou

(Essential poets; 35)
Translated from the Dutch
ISBN 0-920717-01-2 (bound)
ISBN 0-920717-00-4 (pbk.)

I. McGeehan, Charles II. Title.
III. Title: The Gardens of Suzhou. IV. Series.

PT5868.S28F6713 1987 839.3'1164 C87-090263-6

Contents

Formentera

For Thea

per fer una cançó
he tingut bon fonament…

(for the making of a new poem
I've got a grounded reason…)
Catalan Refrain

The Spruce

creeping across the rocks
dry and wrung out
mowed down by the wind
like a dog with its tail
between its legs it grows
back into the stone so
as to keep its head
barely green above water

a goat however all four
legs tethered does jump
over the wall

Almond Trees

in the harsh light
of the wind they move
pink and white
their soft crowns
dream of hard nuts

The Fig Trees

in the round temples
of the fig trees
lie — living altar —
the sheep and sleep
in the eternal repose
which awaits the edge
of the knife

Light at Sea

in regard to that
single light at sea
a ship
all stars are standing still
unless they're falling

deluded by the light
of the single star already
fallen for ages and still
visible
to the naked eye

seeing what's not there anymore
because it is still there

so too is man falling
in a blink of the eyes
into eternity

Evening

in the going
and coming
of ships

and that in
the falling evening

which later crawls up
over lightbulbs
and some candles

in it the lips
burned crusty
ore

still smelting
but in the morning
iron

as
in the coming
and going
of ships

The Visit

an adobe house
the hole is a window
square through that
the sunlight

says the woman
two eggs
one big for
the woman one little
for the man
and gives them

think I
back to
simplicity

the dream picks
itself up
and gives you
for free

Living

living in an
endless house
a window
on space

an old wolf
within this view
turns in his last tooth
wrapped up in a fish

the sheepskin
keeps being sweet
and devoted

short of breath

Leaf 1

a leaf
yellowed hand
shivering taken up
in a wind
unknown
and
      away
later on crunches
shriveled up
under my feet

Leaf 2

when the leaf
fell into its own shadow
it dreamed back
about the branch on which
it hung

The Cave

as swift as
the air is
the sea so
blue

so swiftly in-
to the cave so
black

white foam
snatches
the shoe
so swiftly
forgotten
on the run

Walls

built by men
by time and slow life
the stones gathered
one by one
from the obstinate earth

enclosure for sheep
trees and goats

steaming in the morning
from the sweat
they're still glowing
in the evening
the farmers' bent backs

The Sea

the sea bottles up nothing
spits everything onto land

sometimes in a smooth mirror
she takes a bath

out of that the fisherman
skillfully pulls his fish

Ruffles on the Sea

you step
on a leaf
bird flies off
lizard flees
back into the wall
I see you standing there
for a moment
gone
the wind over sea
is only visible
in the light of
the sun
ruffles on the sea

The Bicycle Repairman

in his cave
dimly lit
one door open
he sits
kneels
and hunkers
before his umpteenth
bicycle

you say hi
he says hi
a twinkling in
his eyes and he sees
upon all these pedals
illuminated all over all
those legs and from the saddle
all those thighs those dresses
blowing up and what's under them
and he has to imagine

then he stands up
clasps the handlebar
can see all those hands
round the handgrip
and gives a tug

then he mumbles:
one day
at noon Mount Mola drifted
into the mist
and became totally invisible

The Fisherman / The Dog

In memoriam: A. Roland Holst

the fisherman lives
alone
with his shadow
his dog
in a hut
alone
by the sea

the fisherman takes
his boat out
at five o'clock
every morning

the fisherman in
his clothes
like the dog
in his skin

together they drift
to the point infinite
where hearing and
seeing are
lost

who's rowing

now the sea alone

at the hottest time of day
fisherman and dog sleeping

in the hut
alone
by the sea

desire bites lonesomely
into the hot sand

Rain

for a moment it seemed
thought the people
it's going to rain

many a glance
moved thirstily
upward

gray clouds
a wild field
black corn-poppies
drifted over
at full speed

what remained was
a hole for
the sun

sighed the people
it'll still be dry awhile

Closed Society

fathers dream of sons
and sons of mothers and
mothers of sons and
daughters of fathers
and sons of other
fathers and mothers and
sons and daughters are
dreams of fathers and
mothers and daughters
and sons girls and
boys loaded with dreams

Noose

on the empty
side of life
hangs a muslin cloth
(Religion)
on a wall
for the bleeding
that unanswered
creeps where no-one
can go
and slowly lifts
itself into its own noose

Zeno

according to Zeno
you're standing still
in every moment
so I'm moving
when I'm standing
still

rushing in eternal
motion the sea

how do you carry off
called out the man
(while falling)
the standstill

Mola Mountain

over Mola Mountain
creeps the moon
the mountain wobbles
in white light a silent
Chinese lantern
mound of Venus
stitched with rugged
black crowns
the trees on
Mola Mountain mound
of Venus

on Mola Mountain
stood one cow
tied under that
single fig tree

over the cow sweeps
in intermittent three-
quarter time (two yesses
one no) the light
of the lighthouse

the cow is ass
and milk and vagina

in the night the cow gets
covered by boys
forced to do so so as
to learn it in the flashes
of the lighthouse's light
intermittent in three-quarter time

twice yes once no the cow
snuffling tied up and
rolling on Mola Mountain

in the night awakes with a start
the priest of Nuestra Sra del Pilar
on the Mola and lights a candle
seen from above and
falling from the mountain
(his dream) in the
immense sea so
deep pouring into
him the Holy Ghost
and the rain...
so dry this land

before his church in
the morning sit
the boys and refresh
their hot dry throats
with the milk of that
one cow on Mola Mountain

Weather and Wind

you live
said the man
by bullshit
to keep life
going

so too
blue girl
sunburned allover
on the beach
rubs oil on the
reverse side of her dream

this action
is as the man sees it
spontaneously embedded
in the whole
of weather and wind
so a form

Birds

a black crow
on the roof and a magpie
shut windows and doors
and stash the silverware

for the gleam
friends a varnish
friends of desire
friends of rapacity
friends the conciliation
friends a smile
which covers up friends
what we do not friends
have in common
that which divides us

The Text

in the text
of the leaf
the nerve is
the heart
the collateral
nerves are
the veins

what remains
in the fall
is the leaf
that dies
yellowed
in the pattern
of nerve and
collateral nerve
with nothing
in between

Autumn

blood-red the lungs
started out green
on bare branches
expose their veins
in the last
breath and die
splendidly in a gust of wind

Up Early

always had to get up early
and a lot of cycling
now and then I
still tend to think
I'm completely gone
from this world
when I'm waking up
and a warmth through me
streams like flying
must be for a bird

against the cold
I take it

Tomorrow

the loneliness of
a writer face to face
with the unwritten page
by now crying
and not knowing
how to dry the tears
and then saying:
try again tomorrow

The Sea of Marmora

he rinses his glans penis
clean in the sea
of Marmora

throws a penny into
the water
and through this speaks
with faraway loves

meeting place of time
and eternity

nevertheless
a penny in the water
of the sea of Marmora

in the back of his head
to have to know
dying as the curiosity
dies

on the sea of Marmora

sharp and shy
in a barn at the sea
he bites his nails
such is the nature whence
the incarcerated are expelled

what remains is
a stay of execution

a color slide of yet another slide
of the sea of Marmora

the way he wrote this
to save both of them
and myself from the same

the truth lies in
the middle where it always
lay

no father no mother
and no-one's heir
part and counterpart become
his heritage

are the seeds of grain coming up?
did you scratch into the ground
to see the first germs?

something is left behind
it's clinging
                    (sinking in)
to the retina
the hand gives something away
a gesture
extension of the escape route
the negative of a
sense-directed reality
an aching head

on the sea of Marmora
which he'd never seen

connects as if
by the wave of a wand
the concrete
the sea of Marmora

sometimes he says Icarus
(soaring)
and draws his hand
battered out of the harbor
(the eye as well)
it stops inside
the clock
(the ear as well)
in the sediment
of a twist of the wrist
(hand scarped)
he caresses old rust
to life and crackles
paper between his fingers
like the bones in his body

on the sea of Marmora

Las Salinas

(the salt pans)

large geometrical eyes
spread out in the sand
blind mirrors
pink and red
blue and grey
exposed
to the uncalled-for
the color

nonetheless: backbone
                                        the salt of life
                                        (a crooked back)
                                        and ten kilos free
                                        for slaughtering
                                        the swine
                                        and tears

such as
that one pair of pants
entirely made to measure
and patched up
(for ten years)
into what they never
were before

Whale

this eye
old whale
(our dream)
which wasn't a fish
(in so much sea)
a delusory form
fooled our eye
in the open sea

The Rock

and the rock
the hard
the solidified

by rain
(liquid)
by trees
(firm)
split
into moraines

a dry falsetto
splits the air

the roots
divide up the rock
into gravel

macadam
for my feet

The Sun

across that path
at sea
across which she
didn't come
she sank
into the sea

Mitjorn

after no frost seen
for a hundred years
hoarfrost
on the beach of Mitjorn

Mitjorn
the midday
the south
mezzo giorno
medio dia

a nightgown
of glaze ice
brittle brocade
crackling under
your feet
as a curse
and then as white
along that seashore
none seen anymore
in a hundred years
on the beach
of Mitjorn

The Word

finding the word
that dies on your lips
and then testing
the wingbeat
of that bird

eyes shut

the fleeting
that wingbeat

The Ear

into the soft ear of the donkey
falls the evening
into the walls the repose
of the sun

falls the shadow longer
and longer
into the languid gesture
of the rising darkness

The Light

at times the light
against the sea
at times the sand
against the light
and we in between

current and undercurrent
a meeting
on a sleeper

The Gardens of Suzhou

For Thea
and the China Delegation

the great wound
of thirst
in the mirror
of the water
Salvador Espriu

Let's go into that immense sea
which overwhelms us and even so
float on our back and see
the sky — feel the wind —
surrounded by water
Frits Staal,
Exploring Mysticism

In May 1985 I was on a working visit to China with a delegation from the Dutch Ministry of Culture. There we visited, among others, the city of Suzhou, northwest of Shanghai. This city lies in the subtropical delta of the Yangtse River. This delta reminds one of the Po River Plains in the vicinity of Venice. And besides the nickname *City of Gardens*, it has also been called *The Venice of the East*.

Dignitaries, magistrates and rich merchants had these gardens laid out. The oldest date about a thousand years back. Most of them, however, have been there for from four to eight hundred years. They were laid out in harmony with the landscape, or, as the Chinese say, they were "borrowed from the landscape." That is, the landscape influences the laying out of the gardens, and the gardens influence and support the landscape. They are *poetic gardens*; also full of poetic names, such as the pavilion that invites you to sit down there and "listen to music when the west wind blows," or "rest here a while and wait for who."

As the garden architects borrowed from the landscape, so the poets have borrowed from the gardens.

Bert Schierbeek

1

the silence
a hole in the
sound in which
she curls up
the fur of a
cat caressed
until sparking

2

making sand heavier
than wind
laying a stone on it
boring into the stone
a hole for the wind

3

the fly of love
hangs in the
spider's web
the night the
names rise on
a silken thread

4

before you know it
you're in needleworked silk

and what isn't stitched in time
suffocates
a sigh rustles
through the trees
on the lips
of many

5

gulls
large white flakes
snowing upwards
in a rain
of darkness

6

eyes blind as
a mirror exposed
to the unasked-for
a storm
three times as much air
in fierce motion

7

water
the fish
of my dreams

a branch defoliates
disinherited
remains nerve

8

so I built a staircase
for somebody else
who climbed up
and kicked me down

9

now they our
occupants kneel
down and say look
our thoughts
we weren't
expecting them

10

this morning
the beach was wearing
a flimsy chemise
of glaze ice

the sun
in the afternoon
slowly pulled her

chemise off
the steaming beloved

11

sitting in this
pavilion and listening
to music when the
west wind blows
voices which contradict
each other
a unity of form

a melody of green
ravines in the shadow
of very old trees
flying forms of great
flat-bottomed skate

hovering elucidating
the face of gravity
and balance

12

o, Mrs Li's father
has died
Mrs Li's father
was a painter and
specialized in
birds and flowers

the world said Mrs Li
and all the gardens thereupon
became colorless and silent
said Mrs Li, very silent

13

Gift

Fu Chai to his wife Xishe
why are you unhappy
I gave you everything but the
moon what more do you want

the moon Xishe calls out

Pi tells his king
dig her a pond

one night
at full moon
Xishe scoops some water
from the pond with her hands
and calls out: look
I have the moon in my hands

14

Parade

the parade of the shoes
full of music in the palace

of the beauties has vanished
Squid Pond
and Fragrant Brook have
dried up in the springtime
only weeds left
the moon shone on things for
ages a token of despair

15

Monsieur Guichet

in his garden
in his slippers
stands he and says:
you were in China and takes
one of his slippers off
and out of that a doubled
up inner sole
(I see his white
moldy instep)

made out of corn-silk
he calls out from China
won't wear out
he calls out

then he sits upon his
stone takes his scythe
hammer and anvil
and pounds away
the way he crushes
the apples into cider

in his mill later on
smiling with his toothless
mouth he calls out
between the hammer beats
on vit bien ici
happier here
than anywhere else
that I don't know

16

The Pond

For Michel van Erkel

in the valley
lies the garden
in the garden
the pond
in the pond
the mountains the trees
the birds
mirror themselves
among the fish
the wrinkled head
of the wind

17

fragrance of tea
three stones

in a sea
of silver

18

above the water
of rippled sand
whistles the wind
deathly still

19

the ship heading upstream
greets the fish heading downstream

20

moon slides
across lake of sand
and takes water

21

current and undercurrent
an encounter
on a cross-tie

22

sometimes the light
against the sea
sometimes the land
against the light
and we in between

23

o the mountain
and the singing
up there
and we
down here

24

so calm the sea
so peaceful but
below that scum
carries on
and comes up

new things he cried out
to write about
as old as the night
she cried out a buzzard
hovering in the air
swoops down upon
a mouse

said he we're going to
abolish history
and ignorance and suffering
and we did that
with much ignorance and suffering

an empty shell
in our hands
filled with ignorance
and with suffering

history was the
only thing we had

like the buzzard
its mouse

25

Landscape

a landscape
that proceeds
step by step
and vanishes
into itself

the way the man
hands behind his
back takes the
range of hills

climbing he came
to his smallest form
stood the highest
walked on
sunk
and arrived

the landscape itself
vanishes step by
step into itself

26

The Trip

certainly
camping at the seashore
lost in the land
desert rose in hand
full of sweat

hot sand rasps the throat
a dream of ice
and winter

what have we done?
put up two walls
of awful water
and we in between

a great storm
of displeasure
with the status quo

uprooted by
self-made lightning

27

The Form

the form found
a sigh escapes
from a wound
a round hole
in hard stone

found where
the eye could reach
possibly inflicted
yet unseen

a last breath
steamed upon
the mirror-smooth pond

28

Palace

this palace is leaning
in my eyes
on an airy bridge
of ruffled water

the fluttering wingbeat
of the roof rises
multicolored over red
walls upon the nest
of this palace

29

Sitting Here and Waiting; for Whom?

look here the tenderness
(recognized)
in the grip of resistance
a camp
yet grabbed with nerve
and all
mapped out
immortal
(trembling)
in this stone
on which I wait

30

A Wall

of course
a wall
a question
an insurmountable plane

yet still rough
    it walks away
    comes back

a structure
    the eye saw
    what the ear heard
    a wall made
    to music
and
raises itself

31

The Flower

After Salvador Espriu

the con-
summate
death
of the
flower
in the
final
light
of the
sun
blood-red

32

says Li:
look
dog sits
on its tail
waits for its bone
rushes off with it

33

says Li:
a pound of feathers
won't fly if
there's no bird inside

34

says Li:
nostalgia

rather look
backwards
than forwards
and rather not
dead either

35

Li: On His Son

he has left us
just like his mother
too young and is traveling
over the world
a soul in search
of its peace
or perhaps just
of those movements
that he shared with
his mother before his
birth

never seeing anything else
but that one mountain in
the south and the sea
around it and the lan-
terns between them
trees moving in
the light and everything
always different

36

as Li has said:

the cave of the clouds
you must write upon them
with stone

and pay attention to the lines
and wrinkles like flowers
dream in their sleep
and awaken from
their slumber full of fragrances

how now
and why
do I humanize
these gardens and
the view here
in the splashing light
of the afternoon
this messenger
of silence

where in Xian
in another temple
Chang Kai-Shek
fled without his pants
into the mountains
and a healthy monkey
hung chattering in the
trees swinging
in a directional wind

37

said Li:
look
from nearly nothing
one falls over

for nearly nothing
one stands up

38

Love

two lips
the same ones
on the ear
of the sea
the same ones
which the wind
bends and breaks
two hearts
in motion
on that power

39

I
said the king
drowned
while swimming
in so many waterways

in the fish
of my eyes

and then again next to
the temple the

aviary in which
all those kings
of birds and also
my ears filled
with their color
and song

while swimming
yet I drowned
in the fish
of my eyes

40

first the blossoms
then the cherries
then eat them
perhaps if the
birds are blind
to red

a magnificent
breadfruit tree full
of birds as as they
sing a green
symphony

o god we thought
at the peak
of the storms
we'll be trans-
formed into
poplars

41

*Four Women of and for Corneille**

attentively lying there she
listens to the message
of the bird a song
of remembrance that
sends thrills through
her body
and satisfies

in front of the window
slipping slowly
past is the cloud
blue across her
red hands
caressing her bird
jealous cat in her back
looks on

green from waking up
on the black sofa
she feeds herself languidly
with the black spider
of the sun

---

*Corneille: COBRA painter

volcano herself among
volcanoes lies she
blue at her flood-tide line
spewing green fire
well thought out
of her body's head

42

The Khan's Garden

when the Khan got word
thus wrote Marco Polo
of the finding of a
very remarkable tree
it didn't matter where
in his immense realm
he would give orders
to dig it out with
roots and all the soil
around it forthwith
and however big or heavy
it might be to convey it
to that hill that he had
built up for plantings
that tree in his plant
collection next to the
pond that originated
from his hill which he
experienced as harmony
and union with the secrets
of nature and man the
making of a 'natural

environment' in which
philosophers could study
the course of life in
the growth blossoming
and withering of flowers
and plants and the falling
of leaves like
generations of people

yet his son Genghis right
after his father's death
lay waste to the old man's
womanly creation

43

the gardens
the spontaneous ones
in my head
step outside
unknown in
mata cactuses and wild
other kinds of vegetation
that slumber deeply under
names and later
melt back on the
tongue and scream
here we are
never away

44

Not a Fish-Story

this eye
of old whale
(our dream)
not a fish-story either
(house of Jonah)
a deceptive form
deceived our eye
in the open sea

45

Bonzai

so small do we
make Nature that we
turn her into a
manageable landscape
within the lines
of our hands

thus millions turn
into people and eat
and have food to eat
together apart

Interview with Bert Schierbeek

Conducted by Pasquale Verdicchio

P.V. The two world wars have played an important role in Dutch literary themes and trends. In fact, your first book, *Revolt against the Past* (1945), is an account of your experiences during the Second World War. Though it was essentially a conventional novel, *Revolt* has been said to contain the germ of what was later to become the *compositional* novel, the collage-type novel with which you gained particular prominence.

B.S. I suppose my first book may have been conventional, but I have always asked myself: what is a conventional novel? For not all conventional novels are alike. Also, in the writing of *Revolt against the Past* I was greatly influenced by Malraux's novel, *La Condition humaine*, and that in itself is not a conventional novel.

The book talks of my war experiences, of the resistance group some friends and I had formed; the others were shot by the Germans and I happened to escape. I had to write it down to get rid of it, to give the whole experience a place. In the process of doing that work I realized how many *histories* I was bringing together; I thought that the best way to get a grip on their realities would be to use the collage method — which was already a given thing, I did not invent it — and to characterize them in some manner.

P.V. The collage approach, very prevalent in your later *compositional* novels, is indeed present in that first novel...

B.S. Of course. Initially I was not sure of how it would work out; I had to try it. Then I really started to research what I could do with this technique. In the meantime I also became editor of a literary journal, *The Word*, and became involved artistically with the group of people associated with it. Collectively we were known as *The Fiftiers* (because it all happened more or less around 1950) and we were distinguishable from previous generations of Dutch writers in that we all showed specific interest in the so-called *world* literatures and art forms.

In fact, it was the study of Dadaism and Surrealism, as sort of liberators of material from its normal context, which gave me the impetus to really use the collage form. At first I kept getting it wrong and I thought, "I cannot write anymore!"

What eventually came out was a book called *The Book Le Cocq*, it was 450 pages long! Unbelievable! From this book I cut out ten stories. I put those stories together and I had the book I wanted to write.

After that, I wrote *The Book I*. With this little title, I meant to say that we must peel back all the *I*'s that have been imposed by fathers, mothers, uncles, aunts, teachers, philosophers, priests, and everyone else who tells us exactly what we should be. It had taken me four years to get on the right track!

P.V. The change you were trying to bring about in the form was also a reflection of a personal change?

B.S. I think that if you change your approach to reality, then this will also affect your writing. How to capture that reality is the question. It was then that I started to make more and more collage type things, because life is not one story but many stories. Some beginning, some ending, some half-way through. I thought the collage form would be the best way to put things together, since you must fall back on the other qualities of language: sound, meaning and sound together, rhythmic qualities, and associate possibilities. Then you have to put these together, in a clear form. In a *compositional* novel it is very important to be selective, you must choose carefully what to cut and what to keep. And typography is important. If there are no chapters, then there must be some other indication to the reader as to how he or she must read.

P.V. What about appearances? The *compositional* novel is termed a novel but it takes on the form of poetry.

B.S. I was using many types of language: poetry, prose, advertisement, all sorts of things. You could use stories that people tell you — I was always listening and writing down what people said, which I would then sometimes use. That was how things started. After a few years I was able to tell from the first few pages whether it would become a thin book, and hence a more poetic one, or a thick one, and thus more like prose.

P.V. It has been said that an important aspect of your work is the attempt to liberate words, to make them *un-things*. How can words ever become detached from the layers of meaning they have acquired?

B.S. You can never liberate a word from its significance; each word has a long history. You can take a word and put it in a context in which it has never been before. This way you are giving it new colour, new sound, new meaning.

P.V. Are you not aiming to subtract all other meanings from a word and bring it down to its primitive state?

B.S. This I would not even try. I think it is impossible. If you see how Joyce uses words — associations, puns, and so on —, you will notice that he is putting them together in different ways and is always changing them. You can always achieve that, give an extra dimension to the reality of things, even in Dutch. With regard to moving from words to *unthings*... a table is a table. But there are some tables with four legs, some with three legs, some with eight legs. When the word *table* acquires such a fixed meaning, what the Dutch call a *begrip* (from *grasping*), then this may become so strong as to disable you from noticing the potentiality of the thing anymore. It is like releasing the tracks a train runs on; taking them and making an iron sculpture extends their possibilities and meaning. The material has been liberated.

P.V. Is this what *The Animal has drawn a Man* (1960) tells us: form born of an unexpected source?

B.S. That an animal should draw a man was not expected. This is a clear *turning around*, a transformation, and thus a very important aspect of the creative process. It is what the Zen Buddhists call *turning your nose*.

P.V. When you say that language is form giving, a medium of composition, do you not then imply, keeping this *turning around* in mind, *decomposition*?

B.S. Decomposition of some sort, but still a composition, since one is putting things in a context other than their normally accepted one. As this happens, so-called normal things become abnormal in their new contextual relationship, and normality then takes on another appearance... Of course, we are limited in what we can do. We have to work with the language that is there; it is a given body of possibilities. That is to say, we are part of the language, but we do not invent it.

P.V. Going back to *The Book I*. You said that form gives a new condition of the self by stripping off all the *I*'s. Is this then an elimination of personal history...? Is personal history a given body of possibilities, like language?

B.S. It is a peeling of all the *I*'s to make the history of your *I* clear. Therefore, it is a giving of form, not an elimination. For the first time you become aware of the kinds of *I*'s you have lived through. My six year old *I* and my present *I* are different, though I hope to have retained part of my younger *I*. It is a way, as it has been described in many religions, of *becoming yourself*. This is a life long process; there will always be some dark part of yourself to discover and explore, and I think this will be evident in each subsequent book.

P.V. In your case, *becoming yourself* seemed to require a movement from *compositional* novels to poetry. Your first book of poems, *The Door*, did not come out until 1972...

B.S. I did not actually begin writing poetry until quite late. Very important for me in the move from prose to poetry was the study of Zen Buddhism during the 1950's and 60's. Zen brings things down to earth. Writing poetry in Dutch is called *dichten* which means to tighten, to make things condensed. The words are stripped of their meaning and they become what they are. No interpretation, just themselves.

P.V. Would you say, then, that the true value of poetry lies in the evolutionary process it underscores?

B.S. The writing of poetry is a very different sort of process than writing a book, one that goes deep into the problems of language itself. In poetry, the word is the diamond, the gem; finding it, along with the proper form of expression, requires a very different approach than does prose. Poetry is a new vision of reality. It discovers and unveils a part of reality never seen before, or at least never seen by the poet.

In poetry, form and content are inseparable; the poet is looking for the form that makes the content. Form should be such that the content is always made new. The same could be said for novels, but I think this is particularly important for poetry.

P.V. Your two books of poetry, *Formentera* and *The Gardens of Suzhou*, seem to illustrate this preoccupation with form and content. Could you comment?

B.S. I tried to let things speak for themselves. By having the form and words reveal a part of Formentera or of the gardens of Suzhou (that could be a fig tree or a pond), by tightening the words down to themselves, they again become part of the landscape and, also, part of us.

P.V. If you were asked to define and place your writing within the context of Dutch literature or of literature in general, where would you situate it?

B.S. In Dutch literature I am still rather an exception. There is no one doing things the way I do, nor has there ever been. This is a fairly unique and strong position to be in. If you want to place me in the so-called *world* literature, then you can say that I have been influenced by several writers: Rabelais, Joyce, Malcolm Lowry, poets like William Carlos Williams and Charles Olson. The main thing is to learn from these authors how to handle the material. This must be done without becoming merely a copy of them, without becoming simply another Joyce.

P.V. There is a tendency to think of experimental or avant-garde writing such as yours as something that will not last. Since your work seems to stand alone even in its experimental category, how would you respond to that view?

B.S. I would say, "Of course it will last!" *The Book I* has sold extremely well, another 25,000 copies had to be printed. While traditions have always been strongest, exceptions have also been allowed to exist.

The Tao of Bert Schierbeek

In the Netherlands Bert Schierbeek is best known for his *compositional* novels. The name refers to a remarkable series of works in which a mixture of prose and verse cross-fertilize each other. They avoid the linear structure of conventional narrative in order to capture some sense of the interconnections between people, events and language, their interdependence in a deeper level of reality. Usually composed in trilogies, they have been appearing since 1951. During the 70s, however, Schierbeek published three collections of verse made up in the main of shorter or longer sequences. These are characterized by a greater simplicity of writing but at the same time retain a complexity of meaning and levels of significance. Selections from all his major books up to this time are available in the anthology of his work, *Shapes of the Voice* (Twayne, 1977). Since then has appeared another trilogy, the second work of which has recently been published under the title *Cross Roads* (Katydid Books, 1988), again in Charles McGeehan's translation. The two verse sequences contained here were written soon after.

Interconnection and interdependence are major themes in Schierbeek's work. It is characteristic of his manner that he prefers to demonstrate rather than write about them, so that a sense of his meaning arises in the reader. In this he is aided by his habits of composition. Some writers keep notebooks; Schierbeek jots down significant images, thoughts, scraps of conversation on separate pieces of paper, whenever they occur to him. Eventually the way into a new work emerges. He then assembles his collage materials and allows his mind to play over them until connections begin to form. Where verse sequences are concerned, much depends on the order in which the fragments appear, and there is a certain amount of rewriting to point up the direction in which his thoughts are moving. There is evidence of this in *Formentera* and *The Gardens of Suzhou*. Sections 21 and 22 of the latter combine as the final poem in *Formentera*; and a slightly different version of "Whale" appears as section 44. There are also back-references to earlier work. Section 8 of *The Gardens of Suzhou* is a reworking of the opening of the second paragraph in *Cross Roads*. "Zeno" in *Formentera* gains in significance in the light of a poem in the sequence "Running and Standing Still" (from *The Way In and Out*, 1974):

the man
moving
(in whichever direction)
creates spaces
no matter how he's moving
(said the man)
and stood still.

In the context of the sequence itself, we have been prepared for "Zeno" by the earlier "Light at Sea". Similarly the bicycle repairman's reference to Mount Mola becomes clearer after we have read "Mount Mola".

It might be useful to bear in mind at the outset that

Schierbeek's singular vision is based on Oriental modes of thought. In 1959 he wrote a series of essays on Zen, probably because he had an intuitional grasp of the subject already. As McGeehan has commented, "even before he'd ever heard of Zen his books were full of Zen". When it was developing in China as the Ch'an school, Zen was most likely influenced by Toaism, that quietistic way of seeing things which was responsible for the harmonious gardens of Suzhou and went on to influence those of the Zen monasteries in Japan. Such points of view are relativistic and anti-Romantic. What you see depends on what you are thinking, not the other way around. This justifies some of the same material appearing in both sequences here. Their meanings are modified by the different preoccupations in the two works.

The poems at the beginning of *Formentera* depict the struggle to transcend conditions. Things and people rise beyond merely battling for existence to a creative fruiting and in that instant are no longer temporary and isolated units; by sharing in an eternal process, they discover eternity in themselves. The Tao (or Eternal Way) entails abandonment of the self-referential vision of the universe and a harmonising with totality. Rather than forcing one's will on nature in the Western manner, everything is valued for itself and understood in its own terms. Not that such thinking is foreign to us; it is the foundation of ecology, which in its turn owes much (in North America at least) to the wisdom of the Indians. "The Visit", as well as celebrating such *primitive* vision, might serve as a commentary on some passage from the *Tao Te Ching*. It looks towards that original state of simplicity which Taoism refers to under the symbol of the uncarved block and which in terms of the Zen koan is "your face before you were born".

of the heart. Schierbeek links with this the folk-tale of how the moon was captured in a handful of water. He is aware at the same time that in Zen the moon is a symbol of Enlightenment, the attainment of oneness. In line with all other mystics, East and West, its teaching is that the seemingly unattainable absolute we yearn for is to be found in the closest and most simple things — in a handful of water, for example, if we will only observe attentively. "The Pond" which reflects everything also derives from a Buddhist parable. What prevent us from realising the harmony we seek are the movements of the fish of our preconceived notions and the gusts of our passions.

The way to still the water of our minds, according to Zen, is *simply sitting*, silently observing the rise and fall of our mental states in detachment. Terminology holds us back, the names which are the shards of the carved block and the private meanings we assign them. Told that the aim is spontaneity, we imitate the Khan in creating artificially a "natural environment". Given our conditioning, it is very hard to arrive at what the Chinese call *wu wei*, actionless action which does not strive after but perceives an already existing harmony; to drop one's self-centred aspirations and discover not a self shut in the centre of self but oneself (the *we* of these poems) open to and at the centre of all things — the process described in "Landscape". What must be given up is the idea of our *self*; certainly it entails a kind of death, but a triumphant one, as both "The Flower" in *The Gardens of Suzhou* and "Autumn" in *Formentera* testify. The hollow it leaves is the hole in the stone that the wind fills; the hollowed stone is no longer what it was, it has become the whole universe.

Yann Lovelock
Birmingham, January 1988.

By the Same Author

1945 *Terreur tegen terreur*
1946 *Gebroken horizon*
1951 *Het boek ik*
1952 *De andere namen*
1955 *De derde persoon*
1957 *De gestatle der stem*
1959 *De tuinen van Zen*
1959 *Het kind der tienduizenden*
1960 *Het dier heeft een mens getekend*
1964 *Ezel mijn bewoner*
1964 *Een broek voor een octopus*
1964 *Een groot dood dier*
1968 *Een grote dorst*
1970 *Inspraak*
1972 *De deur*
1974 *In- en uitgang*
1977 *Vallen en opstaan*
1977 *Weerwerk*
1978 *Schierbeek 2 (Het boek ik / De andere namen / De derde persoon)*
1979 *Schierbeek 1 (Terreur tegen terreur / Gebroken horizon / Het boek Le Cocq)*
1979 *Betrekkingen*

Printed in Canada
at Les presses de l'Imprimerie Saint-Patrice enr.